JAVA

Beginner's Crash Course

Java for Beginner's Guide to Program Java, jQuery & Java Programming.

Table of Contents

Introduction

In the year 1995, Sun Microsystems developed a high level programming language called Java. James Gosling initiated the Java project and released it as a core component of the Sun Microsystems' Java platform. It is the first version of Java called the Java 1.0.

The Java code can work on any device that has the Java virtual machine. Java guarantees its users with the **Write Once, Run Anywhere** concept.

The Java programming language flexible and its Object Oriented concepts are easy to use. Unlike many other programming languages, which got outdated, Java is an ever-evolving language with additional features being added with every new version.

In this tutorial we will be discussing the core concepts and features of Java, with which anyone with a basic knowledge on programming languages can learn Java. We'll discuss the topics step by step with examples making it easy to sink in.

I hope you'll find this book helpful.

Happy reading!!

Chapter 1:
Java Overview

The main features of Java that made it to stand apart from other programming languages are.

Object Oriented: Everything in Java is considered as an object. And because of its Object model it is easy to extend.

Platform independent: When the Java code is compiled, it will be in a platform independent Byte code, which is not the case with other programming languages. This Byte code will be interpreted by the Java virtual machine on the platform where it is being run.

Simple: Java is designed in such a way that it is easy to run. Java can be mastered easily if you know the basic concepts of object-oriented programming.

Secure: tamper free and virus free systems can be developed, thanks to Java 's secure feature. Java uses the public key encryption for authentication techniques.

With Java's secure feature it enables to develop virus-free, tamper-free systems. Authentication techniques are based on public-key encryption.

Architecture-neutral and Portable: The files generated by the Java compiler are architecture neutral object format files. These files can be executed on any processor that can run a Java virtual machine. This makes Java a portable language

Robust: With like runtime checking and compile time checking, error prone situations can be eliminated making Java a robust language

Multithreaded: Java supports the multi thread feature. With multiple threads, programs can smoothly run different tasks at the same time. This helps the developers constructing interactive applications.

Interpreted: The Java byte code can be translated to the native machine language. This will not be stored anywhere. The linking process is Java is a lightweight and incremental process making the development process analytical and more rapid.

High Performance: Java ensures the users with high performance with its Just-In-Time compilers.

Distributed: The design of Java is in such a way that it can be used on the distributed environment of the Internet.

Dynamic: The Java programs are capable of carrying extensive amounts of information during runtime, which in turn can be used for the verification and for resolving access of objects during run-time. This makes a dynamic programming language.

Chapter 2:
Java Basic Syntax

In this chapter we will learn the basic syntax of methods, classes, objects etc. We know that Java is an object oriented programming language, and a program in Java is nothing but a collection of objects. These objects communicate with each other by invoking the other objects methods. Now, we will see what an object, class, instances and methods mean.

Object - Objects have states and behaviors. Example: A car has states - color, name, model as well as behaviors - accelerating, braking, cruising. An object can be defined as an instance of a class.

Class - A class in computers can be defined as a blueprint or a template that describes the states or behaviors that an object supports.

Methods - A method can basically be defined as a behavior. The logic is written inside methods. A class can contain any number of methods. All the actions and data manipulations are executed inside methods.

Instance Variables - every object will have its own unique set of variables. These variables are called as instance variables. These instance variables will have values assigned to them and these are used for defining the state of an object.

Basic Syntax:

When programming in Java, the following points should always be followed.

4

- **Case Sensitivity** - The Java language is case-sensitive. So, one should be careful when writing programs in Java. The words Phoenix and phoenix are not the same and they have different meanings in Java

- **Class Names** - when writing a class name, the first letter should always be an uppercase letter. For example when Car, Bike, Laptop etc. If multiple words are used combine we as a class name, each of those words should be written with the first letter being an uppercase letter. Example *class JavaExampleClass*.

- **Method Names** - when calling a method, the name of that method should always start with a lowercase letter. If multiple words are used to name that method, the first letter of the method will be a lowercase letter and the first letter of the inner words should be in uppercase. Example: *public void exampleJavaMethodName()*

- **Program File Name** - The class name and the program file name should exactly be the same.

- Always remember to save the file using its class name and at the end of the name append '.java'. For example, if the class name is 'BananaNutellaPancake', the file should have the filename '*BananaNutellaPancake.java*'

- **Public static void main (String args[])** - The compiler will start processing the program from the main() method. So, without a main() method it is not possible to write programs in Java.

Chapter 3:
Objects And Classes

Among various types of languages that are present java is classified as an object oriented language. All object oriented languages support the following basic concepts

Polymorphism: It is a case where one object can take up multiple forms. For example "+" can be used for addition as well as concatenation of strings.

Inheritance: It is a case in which the child object gains the properties of its parents.

Encapsulation: It is a case where the data is protected.

Abstraction: It is a case where the class's declaration is completely done but the functionality can be written in different ways using the variables and methods present in the abstract class.

Classes: Objects are created using the class. Class consists of member variables and member functions. It can be considered as a blueprint.

Objects: In object oriented programming objects play a vital role. Objects perform all the functions. They have states in which the variables are and behavior where the variables act in a certain way when they are put into certain methods.

Instance: Instance can be considered as a variable that is declared inside the class but outside the methods of the class.

Method: A method can be considered as a collection of statements that are written to perform a particular task.

Knowing more about the Objects in Java

Any physical thing that you see around you that has physical characteristics can be considered as an object. All these have states and behavior that can be noticed.

All these objects have a state and behavior. These are real world objects now let us consider software objects that have similar states that are shown by variables and behavior that is shown via methods.

Example of Classes in Java:

```
public class Dog{
String breed;
int age;
String color;
void barking(){
}
void hungry(){
}
void sleeping(){
}
}
```

There are multiple types of variables such as local variables, global variables, class variables, instance variables. Depending on the span of the variable's span variables can be divided into local and global variables.

Local variables are defined inside the functions and can be used only inside the functions. In other words local variables are destroyed as soon as the function is completed.

Global variables are defined outside and their scope is last throughout the program.

Instance variables: Instance variables are declared inside the class but outside of the methods. These can be used by all the methods that belong to that specific class only.

Instance variables: Instance variables are variables within a class but outside any method. These variables are instantiated when the class is loaded.

Class variables are variables that are similar to instance variables. The only difference is that they are declared with static keyword.

A class can have multiple variables and methods.

Chapter 4:
Constructors

Constructors play a vital role when it comes to class. Constructors can be explicitly created while creating a class else the java compiler creates a constructor automatically. Every single time an object is created at least one constructor is invoked. A class can have more than one constructor. A constructor should have the same name as the class. Every constructor must have a destructor.

Example of a constructor:

```
public class Puppy{
public Puppy(){
}
public Puppy(String name)
{
    // This constructor has one parameter, name.
}
}
```

Creating an Object

As mentioned previously, a class provides the blueprints for objects. So basically an object is created from a class. In Java, the new key word is used to create new objects.

There are three steps when creating an object from a class:

Declaration: A variable declaration with a variable name with an object type.

Instantiation: The 'new' key word is used to create the object.

Initialization: The 'new' keyword is followed by a call to a constructor. This call initializes the new object.

Example of creating an object is given below:

```
public class Puppy{
public Puppy(String name)
{
   // This constructor has one parameter, name.
   System.out.println("Passed Name is :" + name );
}
public static void main(String []args){
   // Following statement would create an object myPuppy
   Puppy myPuppy = new Puppy( "jimmy" );
}
}
```

If we compile and run the above program, then it would produce the following result:

Passed Name is :jimmy

Accessing Instance Variables and Methods:

Instance variables and methods are accessed via created objects. To access an instance variable the fully qualified path should be as follows:

```
/* First create an object */
ObjectReference = new Constructor();

/* Now call a variable as follows */
ObjectReference.variableName;

/* Now you can call a class method as follows */
ObjectReference.MethodName();
```

Example:

This example explains how to access instance variables and methods of a class:

```java
public class Puppy{
int puppyAge;
public Puppy(String name)
{
   // This constructor has one parameter, name.
   System.out.println("Passed Name is :" + name );
}
public void setAge( int age ){
   puppyAge = age;
}

public int getAge( )
{
   System.out.println("Puppy's age is :" + puppyAge );
   return puppyAge;
}
public static void main(String []args){
   /* Object creation */
   Puppy myPuppy = new Puppy( "jimmy" );

   /* Call class method to set puppy's age */
   myPuppy.setAge( 2 );

   /* Call another class method to get puppy's age */
   myPuppy.getAge( );

   /* You can access instance variable as follows as well */
   System.out.println("Variable Value :" + myPuppy.puppyAge
);
}
```

}

Chapter 5:
Java Package

In simple words, a Java package can be defined as a categorized set of interfaces and classes. Categorizing these classes and interfaces is a must in Java when developing applications as hundreds of interfaces and classes will be used. Categorizing these will make the job easier.

Import statements

A fully qualified name in Java, which contains the class name and the package is passed down to the compiler, the compiler can locate the classes or source code easily. By giving the import statement to the compiler, we are given the location of that particular class.

In this example, this line will tell the compiler to load the classes present in the java_installation/java/io directory.

import java.io.*;

A Simple Case Study

Here, we will create two classes Employee and EmployeeTest for case study.

- Open notepad and write the code given below. You should remember that this is the Employee class and it is a public class.

- Save this file with the name Employee.java.

There are four instance variables present in the employee class namely name, age, designation and salary. This class has also got an explicitly defined constructor. This constructor takes a parameter.

Example:

```java
import java.io.*;
public class Employee{
 String name;
 int age;
 String designation;
 double salary;

 // This is the constructor of the class Employee
 public Employee(String name){
    this.name = name;
 }
 // Assign the age of the Employee  to the variable age.
 public void empAge(int empAge){
    age =  empAge;
 }
 /* Assign the designation to the variable designation.*/
 public void empDesignation(String empDesig){
    designation = empDesig;
 }
 /* Assign the salary to the variable        salary.*/
 public void empSalary(double empSalary){
    salary = empSalary;
 }
 /* Print the Employee details */
 public void printEmployee(){
    System.out.println("Name:"+ name );
    System.out.println("Age:" + age );
    System.out.println("Designation:" + designation );
    System.out.println("Salary:" + salary);
 }
```

```
}
```

As previously mentioned, the process of the program starts only after the main() method. So there should be a main method and a few objects should be present for this Employee class to run. And for these tasks there will be a separate class created.

The *EmployeeTest* class is given below and it creates two instances that belong to the Employee class. These objects invoke the methods for every object and they will assign values for all variables.

Save the given code in the file EmployeeTest.java.

```java
import java.io.*;
public class EmployeeTest{

public static void main(String args[]){
    /* Create two objects using constructor */
    Employee empOne = new Employee("James Smith");
    Employee empTwo = new Employee("Mary Anne");

    // Invoking methods for each object created
    empOne.empAge(26);
    empOne.empDesignation("Senior Software Engineer");
    empOne.empSalary(1000);
    empOne.printEmployee();

    empTwo.empAge(21);
    empTwo.empDesignation("Software Engineer");
    empTwo.empSalary(500);
    empTwo.printEmployee();
}
}
```

Compile both of these classes and run the *EmployeeTest* and it will give the following output.

C :> javac Employee.java

C :> vi EmployeeTest.java

C :> javac EmployeeTest.java

C :> java EmployeeTest

Name:James Smith

Age:26

Designation:Senior Software Engineer

Salary:1000.0

Name:Mary Anne

Age:21

Designation:Software Engineer

Salary:500.0

Chapter 6:
Data Types In Java

Variables can be defined as a result of memory locations that are used for storing values. When you create a variable you're actually reserving memory space on your system.

The operating system will allocate memory basing on the datatype of the variable. The operating system will then decide what can be stored in that memory reserved. Different data types can be assigned to variables allowing you to store characters, integers in these reserved spaces or variables.

In Java, there are two data types available. They are.

- Primitive Data Types

- Reference/Object Data Types

Primitive Data Types:

Java supports eight data types that are primitive. These primitive data types are named by a keyword and are already predefined. Now we will have a look at these eight primitive data types in Java.

byte:

- Byte data type is an 8-bit signed two's complement integer.

- The minimum value of a byte is -128 (-2^7)

- The maximum value of a byte is 127 (inclusive)($2^7 - 1$)

- The default value of a byte is 0

- With the byte data type, space can be saved for a large arrays as it is one fourth of an int.

- Example: byte x= 20, byte y= -46

short:

- Short data type is a 16-bit signed two's complement integer.

- The minimum value that can be stored in a short is -32,768 (-2^{15}).

- The maximum value that can be stored in a short is 32,767 (inclusive) (2^{15} -1).

- The short data type is half the size of an int and twice that of a byte.

- The short data type is also used to save memory.

- Default value of the short is 0.

- Example: short p= 15000, short q= -12000.

int:

- Int data type is a 32-bit signed two's complement integer.

- The minimum value that can be stored in an int is -2,147,483,648.(-2^{31}).

- The maximum value that can be stored in an int is 2,147,483,647(inclusive).(2^{31} -1).

- The int Data type is generally used for storing integer values by default unless there is a concern about the memory being allocated.

- The default value of an int is 0.

- Example: int I= 123000, int j= -150000.

long:

- Long data type is a 64-bit signed two's complement integer.

- The minimum value that can be stored in a long is -9,223,372,036,854,775,808.(-2^63).

- The maximum value that can be stored in a long is 9,223,372,036,854,775,807 (inclusive). (2^63 -1).

- We use the long data type in cases where the range of int is not sufficient.

- The default value of a long is 0L.

- Example: long a = 145600L, int b = -450000L

float:

- Float data type is a single-precision 32-bit IEEE 754 floating point.

- The float data type is mainly used for saving the memory in large arrays where the floating Point numbers are used.

- The default value of a float is 0.0f.

- For storing precise values like currency values, the float datatype is never used.

- Example: float f1 = 213.5f.

double:

- double data type is a double-precision 64-bit IEEE 754 floating point.

- For storing decimal values, the double datatype is generally the default choice.

- The double datatype, just like the float data type, should never be used for storing precise values.

- The default value of a double is 0.0d.

- Example: double d1 = 1234.5

boolean:

- boolean data type represents one bit of information.

- The Boolean data type has only two possible values. True or False.

- This data type is used for true/false conditions.

- The default value of this data type is false.

- Example: boolean one = false.

char:

- char data type is a single 16-bit Unicode character.

- The minimum value that can be stored in a char is
  '\u0000' (or 0).

- The maximum value that can be stored in a char is
  '\uffff' (or 65,535 inclusive).

- Any character can be stored in the char data type.

- Example: char letterA ='A'

Reference Data Types

Using the defined constructors the Java classes, reference
variables can be created.

- Reference variables are used for accessing objects.
  Once these are declared with a data type they cannot
  be changed. For example: Vehicle, Student etc.

- The class objects and different types of array
  variables are all different data types.

- The default value for any given reference variable is
  NULL.

- Any declared are compatible object can be referred
  using the reference variable.

- Example: Vehicle vehicle = new Vehicle("hellcat");

Java Literals

A literal in Java can be defined as the representation of the
source code of a fixed value. Literals are directly represented
without any computation in the code.

For any given primitive type variable, Literals can be assigned. For example:

byte a = 68;

char a = 'A'

The data types byte, short, int and long can be expressed in decimal(base 10), hexadecimal(base 16) or octal(base 8) number systems also.

We use 0 as prefix for indicating an octal and 0x for expressing the value in hexadecimal when these number systems are used for Literals. Here is an example.

int decimal = 100;

int octal = 0144;

int hexa = 0x64;

The string literals in Java are specified just like they are specified in other programming languages. This is done by enclosing a set of characters inside a pair of double quotes. Here are some examples on string Literals.

"Hello World"

"two\nlines"

"\"This is in quotes\""

Only Unicode characters can be given to the string and char data types. For example:

char a = '\u0001';

String a = "\u0001";

Java also supports a few special escape sequences for the char and string Literals. They are:

Notation	Character represented
\n	Newline (0x0a)
\r	Carriage return (0x0d)
\f	Formfeed (0x0c)
\b	Backspace (0x08)
\s	Space (0x20)
\t	tab
\"	Double quote
\'	Single quote
\\	backslash
\ddd	Octal character (ddd)

\uxxxx	Hexadecimal UNICODE character (xxxx)

Chapter 7:
Variables

When a variable is declared, it provides the user with a named storage that the programs can later manipulate. In Java, every variable has a specific type, which in turn determines the layout and size of that variable's memory, the operations that can be performed on that variable and the maximum and minimum values that can be stored within it.

Always remember that you should declare the variables before using them. The basic variable declaration form is given below.

data type variable [= value][, variable [= value] ...] ;

In the example given above, the *data type* is the Java's data type and the name of the variable is *variable*. If you wish to declare multiple variables of the same data type, a comma (,) can be used to separate the list.

Here are a few examples on variable declaration and variable initialization.

int a, b, c;   // Declares three ints, a, b, and c.

int a = 10, b = 10; // Example of initialization

byte B = 22;   // initializes a byte type variable B.

double pi = 3.14159; // declares and assigns a value of PI.

char a = 'a';   // the char variable a iis initialized with value
       'a'

In this topic, we will look at the various variables that are available in Java. In Java, there are three different types of variables.

- Local variables

- Instance variables

- Class/static variables

Local variables

- Local variables are the variables that are declared inside blocks, methods, or constructors.

- Local variables are only available as long as their block, method or constructor is present. Once the block, method or constructor is exited, the local variable will be destroyed.

- We cannot use access modifier is on local variables.

- The local variables can only be seen inside the block or method or constructor in which they are declared.

- Internally, the implementation of local variables will be done at stack level.

- As there are no default values that can be given for local variables, a value should be assigned by declaring them before using them.

Here is an example in which we use local variables.

Example:

Here, *age* is a local variable. This is defined inside *pupAge()* method and its scope is limited to this method only.

```
public class Test{
 public void pupAge(){
   int age = 0;
   age = age + 7;
   System.out.println("Puppy age is : " + age);
 }

 public static void main(String args[]){
   Test test = new Test();
   test.pupAge();
 }
}
```

The above code will produce the following output.

Puppy age is: 7

Example:

In the following example, we are using the *age* variable without initializing it. So during compilation this will give an error.

```
public class Test{
 public void pupAge(){
   int age;
   age = age + 7;
   System.out.println("Puppy age is : " + age);
 }

 public static void main(String args[]){
   Test test = new Test();
```

```
    test.pupAge();
  }
}
```

The following error will be produced by the code during compile time.

Test.java:4:variable number might not have been initialized

age = age + 7;

       ^

1 error

Instance variables

- Instance variables are variables that are declared inside a class but outside a constructor or a method or a block.

- An instance variable value will be created when some space is allocated in the heap memory for an object.

- Whenever we use the **new** keyword for creating a new object, an instance variable will be created along with the object and it will be destroyed along with the object.

- The values that an instance variable hold much be different set by multiple methods, block or constructor. If not, The essential parts of an object's state should prevail throughout the class.

- You can declare instance variables at class level before use or after use.

- Instance variables can have access modifiers.

- In Java, instance variables can be seen by all blocks, constructors and methods that are present in the class. It is advised to make the instance variables private. However, by using access modifiers we can give visibility for the subclasses of these variables.

- The instance variables should be defined during declaration or inside a constructor. If the variables are not defined, the default values of these instance variables will be considered. The default value for numbers is 0, false for booleans and NULL for object references.

- By calling the name of the variable in a class, you can directly access instance variables.

Here is an example.

Example:

import java.io.*;

public class Employee{
// this instance variable is visible for any child class.
public String name;

// salary variable is visible in Employee class only.
private double salary;

// The name variable is assigned in the constructor.
public Employee (String empName){
   name = empName;
}

// The salary variable is assigned a value.

```
public void setSalary(double empSal){
   salary = empSal;
}

// This method prints the employee details.
public void printEmp(){
   System.out.println("name : " + name );
   System.out.println("salary :" + salary);
}

public static void main(String args[]){
   Employee empOne = new Employee("Ransika");
   empOne.setSalary(1000);
   empOne.printEmp();
}
}
```

The program will produce the following output.

name : Ransika

salary :1000.0

Class/static variables:

- Class variables are also called as static variables. These variables are declared by using the *static* keyword inside a class but out of a block, constructor or method.

- Any number of objects can be created from a class variable but there will only be one class variable in a class.

- The class variables are mostly used for being declared as constants. A constant is a variable that is declared as static, public/private and final. As the name suggests, the value of the constant variables remains the same and cannot be changed.

- The class/static variables are stored in the static memory. These variables are rarely used as public or private constants.

- Class variables are created during the starting up a program and they will be destroyed when the program ends.

- The visibility of class variables is similar to the instance variables. However, the static variables are usually declared as public so that other users of that class can use them.

- The default value for numbers is 0, false for Booleans and NULL for object references.

- Values can be assigned to the static variables only during the declaration or inside the constructor. If you wish to add additional values, you can assign them by using the special static initializer blocks.

- By calling the static variables with their class name, you can access them. Syntax: *ClassName.VariableName*.

Here is an example using static variables.

Example:

```
import java.io.*;

public class Employee{
// salary  variable is a private static variable
private static double salary;
```

```java
// DEPARTMENT is a constant
public static final String DEPARTMENT = "Development ";

public static void main(String args[]){
    salary = 1000;
    System.out.println(DEPARTMENT+"average
salary:"+salary);
    }
}
```

The program will produce the following output.

Development average salary:1000

Modifiers

In some situations you might need to change the meaning of some definitions. In such cases you can use modifiers. Modifier said nothing but keywords with which you can change the meaning of a definition. In Java, there are a number of modifiers including the below two.

- Java Access Modifiers

- Non Access Modifiers

For using the modifier you should include keywords within the definition of a variable, method or class. The modifier should be placed in the beginning of the statement as given in the examples below. They are given in *italics*.

```java
public class className {
    // ...
}
```

```
private boolean myFlag;
static final double weeks = 9.5;
protected static final int BOXWIDTH = 42;
public static void main(String[] arguments) {
// body of method
}
```

Access Control Modifiers:

For setting access levels for constructors, variables, classes and methods, Java provides the users with a set of access modifiers. There are four access levels in Java. They are.

- Visible to the package, the default. No modifiers are needed.

- Visible to the class only (private).

- Visible to the world (public).

- Visible to the package and all subclasses (protected).

Non Access Modifiers:

In Java there are a number of non-access modifiers.

- The *static* modifier is used for creating class variables and methods.

- For finalizing the implementation of variables, classes and the methods we use the *final* modifier.

- You can create abstract classes and abstract methods by using the *abstract* modifier.

- For dealing with threads, we use the *volatile* and *synchronized* modifiers.

Chapter 8:
Operators

While programming, you might constantly need to manipulate variables and for that, Java provides the users with a set of operators. All the operators can be divided into the following groups.

- Arithmetic Operators

- Relational Operators

- Bitwise Operators

- Logical Operators

- Assignment Operators

The Arithmetic Operators

The arithmetic operators can be used for dealing with mathematical expressions. All the athletic operators are listed in the table given below.

Here, we will assume that the variable A holds 5 and the variable B holds 10. Then the following expressions will result:

Operator	Description	Example
+	Addition - Adds values on either side of the operator	A + B will give 15

-	Subtraction - Subtracts right hand operand from left hand operand	A - B will give -5
*	Multiplication - Multiplies values on either side of the operator	A * B will give 50
/	Division - Divides left hand operand by right hand operand	B / A will give 2
%	Modulus - Divides left hand operand by right hand operand and returns remainder	B % A will give 0
++	Increment - Increases the value of operand by 1	B++ gives 11
--	Decrement - Decreases the value of operand by 1	B-- gives 9

The Relational Operators

Java supports the following relational operators.

Assume variable A holds 1 and variable B holds 2, then:

Operator	Description	Example

==	This operator will compare both the operands and check if they are equal or not. This will return a true if they are equal.	(A == B) is not true.
!=	This operator will compare both the operands and check if they are equal or not. This will return a true if they are not equal.	(A != B) is true.
>	This operator will compare both the operands and checks if they left operand is greater than the right operand and if the condition is satisfied, this will return a true.	(A > B) is not true.
<	This operator will compare both the operands and checks if they left operand is less than the right operand and if the condition is satisfied, this will return a true.	(A < B) is true.
>=	This operator when compare the left operand and checks if it is greater than or equal to the right operand. This will return a true if the condition is	(A >= B) is not true.

	satisfied.	
<=	This operator when compare the left operand and checks if it is greater than or equal to the right operand. This will return a true if the condition is satisfied.	(A <= B) is true.

The Bitwise Operators

There are several Bitwise operators in Java. These operators can be applied on byte, short, int, long and char data types.

Bitwise operators perform bit by bit operations and work on bits. Let us assume that a=60 and b=13. Their values in binary will be

a = 0011 1100

b = 0000 1101

a&b = 0000 1100

a|b = 0011 1101

a^b = 0011 0001

~a = 1100 0011

Here is a list of all the Bitwise operators in Java.

Operator	Description	Example
&	Binary AND Operator copies a bit to the result if it exists in both operands.	(A & B) will give 12 which is 0000 1100
|	Binary OR Operator copies a bit if it exists in either operand.	(A | B) will give 61 which is 0011 1101
^	Binary XOR Operator copies the bit if it is set in one operand but not both.	(A ^ B) will give 49 which is 0011 0001
~	Binary Ones Complement Operator is unary and has the effect of 'flipping' bits.	(~A) will give -61 which is 1100 0011 in 2's complement form due to a signed binary number.
<<	Binary Left Shift Operator. The left operands value is moved left by the number of bits specified by the right operan	A << 2 will give 240 which is 1111 0000
>>	Binary Right Shift Operator. The left	A >> 2 will give

		15 which is 1111
	operands value is moved right by the number of bits specified by the right operand.	
>>>	Shift right zero fill operator. The left operands value is moved right by the number of bits specified by the right operand and shifted values are filled up with zeros.	A >>>2 will give 15 which is 0000 1111

The Logical Operators

Here is the list of all the logical operators in Java.

Let us assume that A and B are Boolean variables. A holds true and B holds false. Then:

Operator	Description	Example
&&	This is call the AND operator and this will return a true if both the operands hold non-zero values.	(A && B) is false.

||	This is called the OR operator and this will return a true if any of the two operands hold a non-zero value.	(A || B) is true.
!	This is called the logical NOT operator and it is used for reversing the current logical state of the operand on which it is used. If the condition returns a true, the logical NOT operator will make it a false.	!(A && B) is true.

The Assignment Operators

The lists of all the assignment operators that are supported by Java are given in the table below.

Operator	Description	Example
=	This is a simple assignment operator which assigns the value of the right operand to the left operand.	C = A + B will assign value of A + B into C

+=	This is the add AND operator. This operator will add both the operands and will assign the result to the left operand.	C += A is equivalent to C = C + A
-=	This is the subtract AND operator. This operator will subtract the right operands from the left and will assign the result to the left operand.	C -= A is equivalent to C = C - A
*=	This is the multiply AND operand. This will multiply both the operands and the result obtained will be assigned to the left operand.	C *= A is equivalent to C = C * A
/=	This is the divide AND assignment operator. This operator divides the left operand with the right. The obtained result will then be assigned to the left operand.	C /= A is equivalent to C = C / A
%=	This is the modulus AND operator. This operator takes the modulus of both	C %= A is equivalent to C

	the operands and assigns the result to the left operand.	= C % A
<<=	Left shift AND assignment operator	C <<= 2 is same as C = C << 2
>>=	Right shift AND assignment operator	C >>= 2 is same as C = C >> 2
&=	Bitwise AND assignment operator	C &= 2 is same as C = C & 2
^=	bitwise exclusive OR and assignment operator	C ^= 2 is same as C = C ^ 2
|=	bitwise inclusive OR and assignment operator	C |= 2 is same as C = C | 2

Precedence of Java Operators

The grouping of terms in a given expression will be determined by operator precedence. Some operators will have higher precedence over other operators. For example, the multiplication operator will always have a higher precedence when compared to the addition operator. The operators which have higher precedence will be executed first.

The lists of all the operators arranged in accordance to their precedence are given below. The operators that have higher precedence are placed on the top and they go down the table in decreasing order.

Category	Operator	Associativity
Postfix	() [] . (dot operator)	Left to right
Unary	++ -- ! ~	Right to left
Multiplicative	* / %	Left to right
Additive	+ -	Left to right
Shift	>> >>> <<	Left to right
Relational	> >= < <=	Left to right
Equality	== !=	Left to right
Bitwise AND	&	Left to right
Bitwise XOR	^	Left to right
Bitwise OR	|	Left to right
Logical AND	&&	Left to right

Logical OR	||	Left to right
Conditional	?:	Right to left
Assignment	= += -= *= /= %= >>= <<= &= ^= |=	Right to left
Comma	,	Left to right

Chapter 9:
Conditionals

Java provides its users with two types of decision making statements. They are.

- if statements

- switch statements

The if statement

And if statement in Java consists of a Boolean statement. The Boolean statement will have one or multiple statements. These statements will get executed if the condition is satisfied.

Here is the syntax for an *if* statement.

Syntax:

```
if(Boolean_expression)
{
//Statements will execute if the Boolean expression is true
}
```

The given block of code that is inside the *if* statement will only get executed if the Boolean expression returns true. If it returns a false, the control will go to the code that is present after the if statement. Here is an example:

Example:

```
public class Test {

public static void main(String args[]){
    int x = 10;
```

```
   if( x < 20 ){
      System.out.print("This is if statement");
   }
}
}
```

The program will give the following output.

This is if statement

The if...else Statement

After an *if* statement, you can add an optional *else* statement. The code inside the else statement will be executed if the *if* statement is not satisfied. So, in simple terms, if the *if* statement returns a false, the code in the *else* statement will be executed.

Syntax:

Here is the syntax of an if...else statement.

```
if(Boolean_expression){
//Executes when the Boolean expression is true
}else{
//Executes when the Boolean expression is false
}
```

Example:

```
public class Test {

   public static void main(String args[]){
      int x = 30;
```

```
   if( x < 20 ){
      System.out.print("This is if statement");
   }else{
      System.out.print("This is else statement");
   }
 }
 }
```

This code will give the following output.

This is else statement

The if...else if...else Statement

After an if statement, and optional *else if.... else* statement can be added. This statement proves to be useful in situations where various conditions are to be tested.

There are a few points to remember when you are using the if, else if and else statements.

- And if condition can have any number of else conditions and the else condition should always be placed at the end.

- And if statement can be succeeded by any number of else if statements. These statements should always be before the else statement.

- Once the condition of an else if statement is satisfied, the code inside it will be executed and none of the other else if or else statements will be tested.

Syntax:

The syntax of an if...else is:

```
if(Boolean_expression 1){
//Executes when the Boolean expression 1 is true
}else if(Boolean_expression 2){
//Executes when the Boolean expression 2 is true
}else if(Boolean_expression 3){
//Executes when the Boolean expression 3 is true
}else {
//Executes when the none of the above condition is true.
}
```

Example:

```
public class Test {

 public static void main(String args[]){
   int x = 30;

   if( x == 10 ){
     System.out.print("Value of X is 10");
   }else if( x == 20 ){
     System.out.print("Value of X is 20");
   }else if( x == 30 ){
     System.out.print("Value of X is 30");
   }else{
     System.out.print("This is else statement");
   }
 }
}
```

The above code will produce the following output.

Value of X is 30

Nested if...else Statement

A nested if or nested else statements are nothing but which have another statement inside them. A statement is said to be a nested if statement if it contains an if statement inside an if statement. Similarly, the nested else is nothing but an else statement that has another else statement written in it. You can have any number of *if* or *else* statements inside each other.

Syntax:

The syntax for a nested if...else is as follows:

```
if(Boolean_expression 1){
//Executes when the Boolean expression 1 is true
if(Boolean_expression 2){
   //Executes when the Boolean expression 2 is true
}
}
```

You can nest *else if...else* in the similar way as we have nested *if* statement.

Example:

```
public class Test {

public static void main(String args[]){
   int x = 30;
   int y = 10;

   if( x == 30 ){
     if( y == 10 ){
        System.out.print("X = 30 and Y = 10");
     }
```

```
    }
  }
}
```

This code will produce the following output.

X = 30 and Y = 10

The switch statement

Switch statement can be used for testing the equality with a given list of values. Each of those values is called a case. The variable will be compared with each case and tested.

Here is an example.

```
switch(expression){
  case value :
    //Statements
    break; //optional
  case value :
    //Statements
    break; //optional
  //You can have any number of case statements.
  default : //Optional
    //Statements
}
```

The set of rules given below apply to a switch statement.

- The byte, short, int and char are the only variables that can be used in a switch statement.

- The number of case statements for a switch statement is not limited to one. It can have multiple case statements and there is no limit to it. Each case will have a value with which it will be compared and a colon at the end.

- The switch variable and the value of the case should be of the same data type.

- The switch variable and the case datatype should be literal or a constant.

- If the switch variable and the case are equal, the statement that are present after the case will continue to execute till the control finds a *break* statement.

- This *switch* terminates after the control reaching the *break* statement. The control now goes to the following line that is present after the switch statement.

- It is not compulsory for a case to have a break. If there is no break given, the control will *fall through* subsequent cases till it reaches a break.

- You can add an optional default case for a given switch statement. This option in case should be the last line of the switch. This default case will get executed if none of the above cases are satisfied. When using the default case, you don't need to add *break*.

Here is an example.

Example:

public class Test {

public static void main(String args[]){
   //char grade = args[0].charAt(0);

```java
        char grade = 'C';

        switch(grade)
        {
          case 'A' :
            System.out.println("Excellent!");
            break;
          case 'B' :
          case 'C' :
            System.out.println("Well done");
            break;
          case 'D' :
            System.out.println("You passed");
          case 'F' :
            System.out.println("Better try again");
            break;
          default :
            System.out.println("Invalid grade");
        }
        System.out.println("Your grade is " + grade);
    }
}
```

Compiling and running the program with various command line arguments will give the following output.

$ java Test

Well done

Your grade is a C

$

Chapter 10:
Exceptions

An exception can be defined as the problem that disrupts the normal flow of execution. In simple words it can be defined as a problem occurred during the program's execution. There are many reasons that cause an exception to occur. Some of them are:

- Giving invalid data.

- The Java virtual machine running out of memory.

- Network connection termination during communication.

- The required files cannot be found.

Some exceptions are caused due to the human errors, others due to the programmer errors and the rest due to the failure of physical resources.

In Java, there are three categories of exceptions. For you to understand the concept of exception handling you should know the type of exceptions. The different categories of exceptions are given below.

- **Checked exceptions:** An exception can be defined as a checked exception if it can't be foreseen by the programmer or if it is an typical user error. Checked exceptions cannot be ignored during compilation time.

- **Runtime exceptions:** runtime exceptions can be defined as exceptions that could have probably been solved by the programmer. Runtime exceptions, unlike checked exceptions will be ignored during compilation time.

- **Errors:** Errors can be defined as problems that an user or a programmer cannot control. These cannot be considered as exceptions. Errors are usually ignored as they cannot be solved. For example, an error will be raised in case of a stack overflow. This error will be ignored during the compilation of the program.

The list of the most commonly seen exceptions, both checked and unchecked are given below. All these exceptions are a subset of the **Java's Built-in Exceptions**.

Exceptions Methods

The list of all the important methods that are available from the throwable class are given below.

SN	Methods with Description
1	**public String getMessage()** This method will return a message about the occurred exception in detail and will be initialised inside the constructor **Throwable**.
2	**public Throwable getCause()** This method will return because which made the exception a car and this is represented by a

Throwable object.

3 public String toString()

This message will return the concatenated class name with the result of getMessage().

4 public void printStackTrace()

This method will print the result of the toString() combined with the stack tree to the error output stream System.err.

5 public StackTraceElement [] getStackTrace()

This method will return an array that contains every element on the given stack trace. The element present at the index 0 represents the starting on top of the given call stack while the method present at the bottom of a call stack will be represented by last element that is present in the array.

6 public Throwable fillInStackTrace()

With this method, the stack trace will be filled with this Throwable object with the current stack trace. With this previous information will be added in the stack trace.

Catching Exceptions

In Java, an exception can be caught by a method using the **try** and **catch** keywords. If there is a block of code that might give an exception, it will be placed inside the try/catch blocks. Any code that is placed between the try/catch blocks will be considered as protected code. The syntax for writing the try/catch blocks is given below.

Syntax:

```
try
{
//Protected code
}catch(ExceptionName e1)
{
//Catch block
}
```

When writing a catch statement, the type of exception that you wish to catch should be declared. If there is an exception raised in the protected block of code, the catch block following the try block will be checked. If the exception type is it declared in the garage block, the exception that is passed to the garage block is like an argument that is passed to all method parameter. Here is an example.

Example:

The following program contains an array that has 2 elements. The code is trying to access the undeclared 3rd element making it throw an exception.

```
// File Name : ExcepTest.java
import java.io.*;
public class ExcepTest{
```

```java
public static void main(String args[]){
  try{
    int a[] = new int[2];
    System.out.println("Access element three :" + a[3]);
  }catch(ArrayIndexOutOfBoundsException e){
    System.out.println("Exception thrown  :" + e);
  }
  System.out.println("Out of the block");
}
}
```

The code will produce the following output:

Exception   thrown
 :java.lang.ArrayIndexOutOfBoundsException: 3

Out of the block

Multiple catch Blocks

The number of catch blocks after a try block is not limited to 1. You can have any number of catch blocks following a try block. In real situations, you will have to write multiple catch blocks for efficient exception handling. The syntax for writing multiple catch blocks is given below.

Syntax:

```java
try
{
//Protected code
}catch(ExceptionType1 e1)
{
//Catch block
```

```
}catch(ExceptionType2 e2)
{
//Catch block
}catch(ExceptionType3 e3)
{
//Catch block
}
```

In this example there are three catch blocks after a try block, but you can have multiple catch blocks after a single try block. If there is an exception in the protected god, that will be thrown to the following catch block. If the exception thrown matches the data type ExceptionType1, the exception will be caught there. If the exception data type doesn't match, it will be passed to the next catch block. This process continues till the thrown exception is caught or till all the catch blocks leave the exception. In such cases, the current method will stop the execution and the exception will then be thrown to the previous method on the call stack. Here is an example.

Example:

In this code segment, we will look at multiple try/catch blocks.

```
try
{
file = new FileInputStream(fileName);
x = (byte) file.read();
}catch(IOException i)
{
i.printStackTrace();
return -1;
}catch(FileNotFoundException f) //Not valid!
{
```

```
 f.printStackTrace();
 return -1;
}
```

Example 2:

```
package com.myjava.exceptions;

import java.net.MalformedURLException;
import java.net.URL;

public class MyMultipleCatchBlocks {

  public static void main(String a[]){
     MyMultipleCatchBlocks mmcb = new
MyMultipleCatchBlocks();
     mmcb.execute(1);
     mmcb.execute(2);
  }

  public void execute(int i){
     try{
        if(i == 1){
           getIntValue("7u");
        } else {
           getUrlObj("www.junksite.com");
        }
     } catch (NumberFormatException nfe){
        System.out.println("Inside NumberFormatException...
"+nfe.getMessage());
     } catch (MalformedURLException mue){
        System.out.println("Inside MalformedURLException...
"+mue.getMessage());
     } catch (Exception ex){
```

```java
        System.out.println("Inside Exception...
"+ex.getMessage());
    }
}
  public int getIntValue(String num){
    return Integer.parseInt(num);
  }


  public URL getUrlObj(String urlStr) throws
MalformedURLException{
    return new URL(urlStr);
  }
}
```

The throw/throws Keywords

If the given method leaves the exception doesn't handle the given checked exception, it must be declared with the keyword **throws**. This keyword will be used at the end of a given method's signature.

Using the **throw** keyword, newly instantiated exceptions or exceptions that were just caught can be handled. There is a difference between the **throw** and **throws** keywords.

In the following example RemoteException will be thrown by the method.

```java
import java.io.*;
public class className
{
public void deposit(double amount) throws RemoteException
{
  // Method implementation
  throw new RemoteException();
```

```
}
//Remainder of class definition
}
```

A method can declare that it throws more than one exception, in which case the exceptions are declared in a list separated by commas. For example, the following method declares that it throws a RemoteException and an InsufficientFundsException:

```
import java.io.*;
public class className
{
public void withdraw(double amount) throws
RemoteException,
                InsufficientFundsException
{
   // Method implementation
}
//Remainder of class definition
}
```

The finally Keyword

The finally keyword is used to create a block of code that follows a try block. A finally block of code always executes, whether or not an exception has occurred.

Using a finally block allows you to run any cleanup-type statements that you want to execute, no matter what happens in the protected code.

A finally block appears at the end of the catch blocks and has the following syntax:

```
try
{
//Protected code
}catch(ExceptionType1 e1)
{
//Catch block
}catch(ExceptionType2 e2)
{
//Catch block
}catch(ExceptionType3 e3)
{
//Catch block
}finally
{
//The finally block always executes.
}
```

Example:

```
public class ExcepTest{

public static void main(String args[]){
   int a[] = new int[2];
   try{
     System.out.println("Access element three :" + a[3]);
   }catch(ArrayIndexOutOfBoundsException e){
     System.out.println("Exception thrown  :" + e);
   }
   finally{
     a[0] = 6;
     System.out.println("First element value: " +a[0]);
     System.out.println("The finally statement is executed");
   }
 }
}
```

This would produce the following result:

Exception   thrown
:java.lang.ArrayIndexOutOfBoundsException: 3

First element value: 6

The finally statement is executed

Note the following:

- A catch clause cannot exist without a try statement.

- It is not compulsory to have finally clauses whenever a try/catch block is present.

- The try block cannot be present without either catch clause or finally clause.

- Any code cannot be present in between the try, catch, finally blocks.

Here are some more examples on exception handling.

Example 1: Try- Catch blocks

```
package com.myjava.exceptions;
public class MyExceptionHandle {
  public static void main(String a[]){
    try{
      for(int i=5;i>=0;i--){
        System.out.println(10/i);
      }
    } catch(Exception ex){
      System.out.println("Exception Message: "+ex.getMessage());
      ex.printStackTrace();
```

```
    }
    System.out.println("After for loop...");
  }
}
```

Output

2

2

3

5

10

Exception Message: / by zero

java.lang.ArithmeticException: / by zero

    at
com.myjava.exceptions.MyExceptionHandle.main(MyExcepti
onHandle.java:12)

After for loop...

Example 2: Throws Clause

package com.myjava.exceptions;

```
public class MyThrowsClause {
  public static void main(String a[]){
    MyThrowsClause mytc = new MyThrowsClause();
    try{
```

```
      for(int i=0; i<5; i++){
         mytc.getJunk();
         System.out.println(i);
      }
   } catch (InterruptedException iex){
      iex.printStackTrace();
   }
}

public void getJunk() throws InterruptedException {
   Thread.sleep(1000);
}
}
```

Example 3: Throw clause
package com.myjava.exceptions;

```
public class MyExplicitThrow {
 public static void main(String a[]){
    try{
       MyExplicitThrow met = new MyExplicitThrow();
       System.out.println("length of DUKE is
"+met.getStringSize("JUNK"));
       System.out.println("length of DUCATI is
"+met.getStringSize("WRONG"));
       System.out.println("length of null string is
"+met.getStringSize(null));
    } catch (Exception ex){
       System.out.println("Exception message:
"+ex.getMessage());
    }
 }

 public int getStringSize(String str) throws Exception{
```

```
    if(str == null){
        throw new Exception("String input is null");
    }
    return str.length();
  }
}
```

Output:

length of DUKE is 4

length of DUCATI is 6

Exception message: String input is null

User-defined Exceptions

You can create your own exceptions in Java. Keep the following points in mind when writing your own exception classes:

- All exceptions must be a child of Throwable.

- If you want to write a checked exception that is automatically enforced by the Handle or Declare Rule, you need to extend the Exception class.

- If you want to write a runtime exception, you need to extend the RuntimeException class.

We can define our own Exception class as below:

```
class MyException extends Exception{

}
```

You just need to extend the Exception class to create your own Exception class. These are considered to be checked exceptions. The following InsufficientFundsException class is a user-defined exception that extends the Exception class, making it a checked exception. An exception class is like any other class, containing useful fields and methods.

Example:

```java
// File Name InsufficientFundsException.java
import java.io.*;

public class InsufficientFundsException extends Exception
{
private double amount;
public InsufficientFundsException(double amount)
{
  this.amount = amount;
}
public double getAmount()
{
  return amount;
}
}
```

To demonstrate using our user-defined exception, the following CheckingAccount class contains a withdraw() method that throws an InsufficientFundsException.

```java
// File Name CheckingAccount.java
import java.io.*;

public class CheckingAccount
{
private double balance;
```

```java
private int number;
public CheckingAccount(int number)
{
  this.number = number;
}
public void deposit(double amount)
{
  balance += amount;
}
public void withdraw(double amount) throws
              InsufficientFundsException
{
  if(amount <= balance)
  {
    balance -= amount;
  }
  else
  {
    double needs = amount - balance;
    throw new InsufficientFundsException(needs);
  }
}
public double getBalance()
{
  return balance;
}
public int getNumber()
{
  return number;
}
}
```

In the following program BankDemo, the deposit() and withdraw() methods Will be invoked. They belong to the CheckingAccount.

```java
// File Name BankDemo.java
public class BankDemo
{
public static void main(String [] args)
{
  CheckingAccount c = new CheckingAccount(101);
  System.out.println("Depositing $500...");
  c.deposit(500.00);
  try
  {
    System.out.println("\nWithdrawing $100...");
    c.withdraw(100.00);
    System.out.println("\nWithdrawing $600...");
    c.withdraw(600.00);
  }catch(InsufficientFundsException e)
  {
    System.out.println("Sorry, but you are short $"
                + e.getAmount());
    e.printStackTrace();
  }
 }
}
```

Compiling the above files and running the BankDemo will give us the following output.

Depositing $500...

Withdrawing $100...

Withdrawing $600...

Sorry, but you are short $200.0

InsufficientFundsException

   at CheckingAccount.withdraw(CheckingAccount.java:25)

   at BankDemo.main(BankDemo.java:13)

Common Exceptions

We have two types of errors and exceptions in Java. They are.

- **JVM Exceptions:** JVM exceptions are nothing but the errors on exceptions that are logically or exclusively thrown by the Java virtual machine. Example: ArrayIndexOutOfBoundsException, NullPointerException, ClassCastException, etc.,

- **Programmatic exceptions:** programmatic exceptions can be defined as the exceptions that are thrown by the API or by the application. Example: IllegalStateException, IllegalArgumentException, etc,.

Chapter 11:
How to Install Java

Now that you know what Java consists of, it's time to install it on your computer and look at actually using it. You will need a computer or laptop running Windows, Linux, OS X or Solaris for this.

How to Install Java on Windows

With Windows you can download and install Java both online or offline.

Online

Downloading Java online will result in an Install From The Web (IFTW) executable file being downloaded and this requires the absolute minimum of intervention from you. Running this program will allow all the required files to be pulled in from the web so it is important that you stay connected to the internet throughout the installation process.

- You will require Administrative permissions in order to install Java onto Microsoft Windows

- If you have any trouble with this method, try the offline method, which I will detail after this one.

Installation

- For Windows 2008 Server, 7, 8/8.1, XP, Server 2012, Vista, Windows 10

Before you begin with the installation, disable your firewall. Some ae se to reject any online or automatic installations, like Java and, if the firewall is on or not configured correctly it can hold the download up or stop it altogether.

- Open the <u>Manual download</u> page

- Click **Windows Online**

- A window will appear with the option of running or saving the file – click on **Run** if you want to go ahead with the installation now – if you prefer to do it later, click on **Save** and make a note of where it is saved

- If you click on Run now, the installation process will start straightaway

- Click on **Install** to accept the licensing terms and to go on with the process

- You may be presented with offers of various programs to install during the Java installation – this is because of a partnership between Oracle and several other companies. If you want to install any of them, make sure they are ticked and click on **Next**

- Follow the on-screen directions to complete the installation and, on the last dialog window, click on **Close**. This will finish the installation

Integrated into the installer is an Uninstall program. The idea of this is to detect and remove older versions of Java that may be installed on your computer. This works on both Windows 32 and 64-bit systems.

The installer will also tell you if Java content has been turned off in your web browsers and will give you instructions to follow on enabling it. If you chose to hide security prompts for Java Web Start applications and applets, you will also be given instructions on how to restore those prompts. You may need to reboot your computer if you don't restart a browser when requested to do so.

Offline

This method involves the download of an executable file, which has all of the files that you will need, so that you can install Java in your own time. You will not need to be connected to the internet for the installation, only for the initial download. You can also copy the file and then install it on anther computer that isn't connected to the network.

Again, you do require Administrative permissions to do this.

- Open the <u>Manual download</u> page

- Click on **Windows Offline**

- A dialog window appears, click on **Save**

- Make sure you save the file somewhere easy to locate, such as you desktop

- Close down your browser and any other application that may be running

- When you ae ready to install, double-click the file

- The process will begin, click on **Install** to accept the terms and carry on with the installation

- Again, you may be offered various other programs to install; choose the ones you want, if any, and click on **Next**

- Follow the on-screen directions for completion, clicking on **Close** on the las window to complete the installation.

As with the online method, the uninstall tool will detect older versions of Java and remove them and will also provide you with instructions to enable Java content in your browsers if it has been previously disabled. Instructions will also be given to enable to prompts for applets and Java Web Start applications.

How to Install Java on Mac OS X

Java can be installed on any Mac running OS X 10.7.3 with a 64-bit browser – Firefox or Safari, for example. 32-bit browsers are NOT supported. You will need Administrator permissions

- Download this file – **jre-8u60-macosx-x64.dmg** – don't forget to accept the license terms first

- Double click on the file to start the process

- Double click the package icon – this will launch the installation wizard

- On the Welcome scree that appears, click on **Next**

- Choose any, all or none of the optional programs that are presented to you then click on **Next**

- Follow the on-screen instructions to complete the installation

- Click on **Close** on the final confirmation screen to complete the installation

The same applies to Mac as it does to Windows – if you have disabled Java content in your browsers and/or disabled the prompts for applets and Java Web Start applications, instructions will be provided on how to enable them.

How to Download Java on Linux

There are two packages to choose from here:

- Linux platforms – an archive binary file that anyone can download, in any location that is writeable. Only a ROOT USER can download Java to the system location though

- RPM-based Linux platforms – for 32-bit RPM-based Linux platforms, which have an RPM binary file in the system location – this can only be done by ROOT USERS.

Make sure you choose the package that matches your system and privileges. This will work on Linux Red Hat, SUSE, Oracle, Oracle Enterprise and SLES

- Open **http://java.com**

- Click on **Download**

- Choose the right package to suit your requirements

- Note the size of the file before you download and, once the download is complete, check that the full package has downloaded.

Linux Platforms

For the purposes of this, we are using v7 – make sure you use the version numbers that correspond with what you have downloaded

Open the terminal and change to the relevant directory, the one you want to install Java to by typing:

- cd *<directory path name>* - type in the name of the relevant directory

- Locate the .tar.gz archive binary and move it to the new directory

- Unpack tarball and install Java – ***tar zxvf jre-7u7-linux-1586.tar.gz***

You will find the Java files in a directory named **jre1.7._.07**, which you will find in the current directory

- Delete the file ending **.tar.gz** if you want more disk space

RPM-based Linux Platforms

Again, I am using v7 so make sure you use the correct numbers for your particular version when you are typing in the commands

- Become a root user by running **su** at the command line and then inputting the super-user password

- Remove any older versions of Java from your computer – **rpm –e <*package name*>**

- Change to the directory you are installing Java in – **cd <*directory path name*>**

- Install the java package by typing – ***rpm –jvh jre-7u7-linux-1586.rpm***

- If you want to save a bit of disk space, delete the .rpm file

- Exit out of Shell boot – you do not need to reboot your computer

The installation is finished, now you need to head over to the **Enable and Configure** section

Enable and Configure

Firefox Browser

- Close down the Firefox browser if it is open and running

- Remove any previous Java plugin versions – you can only run one version at a time. If you want to run a different version or a different plugin, you have to remove the symbolic link to other versions and create a new one to the new version

- Create the symbolic link to **libnpjp2.so** – you will find this in the browser plugin directory

    - Look for the sub-directory under the installation directory by typing **cd *<firefox installation directory>*/plugins** (type in the right name for the directory)

    - Create the symbolic link - **ln -s *<Java installation directory>*/lib/i386/libnpjp2.so**

If you are upgrading from an older Java version, you must remove the existing symbolic link before you make a new one:

- Type in **cd** *<Firefox installation directory>*/plugins rm libjavaplugin_oji.so

For example:

- If Firefox has been installed at **usr/lib/<*Firefox installation directory>***

- And Java is at **/usr/java/<*Java installation directory>***

- Then you would type into the terminal window **/usr/lib/<Firefox installation directory>/plugins** to go to the browser plugin directory

- To create the symbolic link to the Firefox Java plug in, type in **ln -s /usr/java/<*Java installation directory*>/lib/i386/libnpjp2.so**

Restart your Firefox browser and, in the Location bar, type in **about: plugins** – this will confirm that the Java Plugin has been loaded in. Click on the Tools menu to make sure that Java console is in there

How to Install Java on Solaris

There are two ways to download Java onto Solaris:

- Solaris SPARC for 32-bit systems

- Solaris SPARC for 64-bit systems

Java is a self-extracting binary file so make sure you download the right package for your system

As with the previous tutorial, I am using v7 for this so be sure that you use the correct version number in any commands that you type.

The JRE archive binary can be downloaded into any location that you can write to and it will not displace the version that has been provided by Oracle Solaris OS.

If you are installing this on a 64-bit system that allows the use of a 32-bit JVM, there are two steps to the process. First, you must install the 32-bit version and then the support for the 64-bit operations. File names are:

On SPARC processors:

- jre-7u7-solaris-sparc.tar.gz (32-bit)

- jre-7u7-solaris-sparcv9.tar.gz (64-bit)

On x64/EM64T processors:

- jre-7u7-solaris-i586.tar.gz (32-bit)

- jre-7u7-solaris-x64.tar.gz (64-bit)

If you are on the 32-bit Solaris, you only have to download the 32-bit version

- Open http://java.com

- Click on **Free Java Download**

- You will see a page with the Manual downloads on it – download the relevant bundles

If you are running a 32-bit version of Oracle Solaris, you only need to download and install the 32-bit version.

Note – the.tar.gz file is also called a tarball and can be uncompressed and extracted in one go

- Change the directory to where the JRE is going to be installed: **cd <*directory path name*>**

- Move the archive binaries ending .tar.gz to the current directory

- Unpack the tarball and install Java:

On a SPARC processor;

- gzip -dc jre-7u7-solaris-sparc.tar.gz | tar xf –

- gzip -dc jre-7u7-solaris-sparcv9.tar.gz | tar xf –

On an x64/EM64T processor

- gzip -dc jre-7u7-solaris-i586.tar.gz | tar xf –

- gzip -dc jre-7u7-solaris-x64.tar.gz | tar xf –

Java will be installed into a directory called jre1.7.0_<*version*> within the current directory and the supplemental 64-bit files will be installed in directories with names that correspond to the machine architecture model. These will be in a number of locations inside the version directory, for example;

SPARC processors – the libjvm.so file (64-bit Java VM library   file)
Java is installed in a directory called jre1.7.0_<*version*> in the current directory.

Enable and Configure

Once you have installed Java, it's time to make sure it is configured to run the applets in your browser:

- Look for the sub-directory for the plugins in the Firefox installation directory by typing **cd <Firefox installation directory>/plugins**

- In the current directory, you need to create a symbolic link to Java libnpjp2.so by typing the following – SPARC processor - **ln -s <Java installation directory>/lib/sparc/libnpjp2.so** . and for x86 - **ln -s <Java installation directory>/lib/sparc/i386/libnpjp2.so** .

You must ensure that you include the period (.) at the end

For example:

- If Firefox is installed at /usr/lib/mozilla-1.4/

- And Java is installed at **/usr/java/jre7u3**

- To go to the browser plugin library you should type this at the terminal - **cd /usr/lib/mozilla-1.4/plugins**

- To create the symbolic link, type in **ln -s /usr/java/jre1.7.0_u<version>/lib/libnpjp2.so**

Restart your Firefox browser and go to the **Edit** menu. Click on **Preferences, Advanced Category** and then click on **Enable Java.** Java will now be enabled for the Firefox bowser.

Chapter 12:
Writing Your First Java Program

So, now that you know about Java and you know how to install it, it's time to start writing programs. Remember that with Java, all the work is done in the Word Processor, NOT at the command line. Open up the Word Processor and type in:

- class Pythagorean {

- public static void main(String[] args){

- }

- }

Let me just explain what you have done here:

Each class opens up inside a new class. Think of a class as a set of instructions or, let's say a recipe for example. Some recipes will need additional recipes for the dish o be completed while others, like the one you have just written, will work on their own. Lett's say you were making guacamole; your recipe would contain step-by-step instructions on how to make guacamole. This is one single class. Now let's assume that you wanted to make a burrito and it needed guacamole in it. Now you have two options – write one recipe that has instructions to make the burrito and the guacamole or you could write the burrito recipe and then add a reference to the separate guacamole recipe. This is what Java does. You can have one class that references another class or you could have one class that contains everything you need. This is why Java is object-oriented – because you write what suits your preference. So, let's break down what you just typed in:

- The name of the class in this case is **Pythagorean.** All Java has to be saved as the name of the class, followed by .java

- The class is opened up by the first {

- The next line, **public static void main(String[]args){** is calling the main method of the class. Although is a little advanced, you should remember this because it is something you will use a lot.

- The } bracket closes the program subdivision. One thing you must do with every program is ensure that every opening bracket has a corresponding closing bracket.

At this stage, your application isn't going to do anything but we need to save it anyway. All java applications should be saved in plain text format

Next, we want to run this application, even though it doesn't do anything. The reason for this is to get you into the habit of doing this. You run your application at each stage just to test it out. So:

Windows:

- Open the command line

- Find where you saved your application

- Now type in to the command line something similar to this: **C:/java/samples>javac Pythagorean.java**

/java/samples is the directory that you are working in. In computer language, */name* signifies a folder. The final part is where you saved your application. If you saved it to your desktop, for example, you would type **/desktop>javac Pythagorean.java**

Javac means java compile and this is a process whereby the application is transformed from readable words into computer language. This is also where many errors, if there are any, will show up. These errors can easily be corrected in the original application.

OK, so if nothing happened then you know your application worked, because it wasn't meant to do anything. Locate the folder that you saved your application in; you should now see a second file that reads **Pythagorean.class.** If it is there, all well and good. If it isn't, you need to check the text in the application and on the command line to ensure that you did everything right.

Mac

This is a similar process to Windows:

- Open up terminal.app

- Locate where you saved your application

- Type in at the terminal **cd *<name of directory>***

- Now type in something along the same lines as you did with the Windows version - **C:/java/samples>javac Pythagorean.java**

The next step is to make your application do something. In your Word Processor window, type in the following (I have started from scratch here but you can continue after what you type earlier, starting from the right place:

- class Pythagorean {

- public static void main(String[] args){

- String greeting = "Hello. Welcome to the Pythagorean Theorem Application. Today we will be computing the Pythagorean Theorem for you.",

- String prompt = "Please enter a number for the first leg of a right triangle, followed by pressing ENTER or RETURN, followed by the remaining leg. Then hit ENTER or RETURN one more time.";

- System.out.println(greeting);

- System.out.println(prompt);

- }

- }

To break that down:

- A string is a line of text and this is known as a variable, which means it can be varied

- Prompt and greeting are the string names so in the line that starts "String greeting" you are making a string that is called "greeting". Note that the line ends with a semicolon – this is important – ALL JAVA STATEMENTS MUST END IN A SEMICOLON otherwise you will get errors

- = is used to assign a value to the variable, which is done like this: **String greeting = "Hello. Welcome to the Pythagorean Theorem Application. Today we will be computing the Pythagorean Theorem for you.";** , or, like this: **String greeting; greeting = "Hello. Welcome to the Pythagorean Theorem Application. Today we will be computing the Pythagorean Theorem for you.";**

In the latter case you are both declaring and assigning value to the variable in two separate steps while, in the first case, you are using just one step. Both work the same way. Keep in mind that all of the text that goes into the variable must be enclosed in quote mark – """

In the line **System.out.println,** you are calling for the system output to print the variable line. If you were to call **System.out.printIn("HI"),** the word "HI" would be printed to your terminal. Note the quote marks here – these indicate that what is in between them in text, not a variable name. If you were to call **System.out.printIn(HI),** without the quote marks, you would get an error message because the program would be looking to print the value of a variable called HI – there isn't one. Commit this command to memory; it is another that you will use constantly.

Now we are going to change things up a little and get a bit more complicated. Change the code you have written so far to say this:

- import java.util.Scanner;

- class Pythagorean {

- public static void main(String[] args){

- String greeting = "Hello. Welcome to the Pythagorean Theorem Application. Today we will be computing the Pythagorean Theorem for you.";

- String prompt = "Please enter a number for the first leg of a right triangle, followed by pressing ENTER or RETURN, followed by the remaining leg. Then hit ENTER or RETURN one more time.";

- System.out.println(greeting);

- System.out.println(prompt);

- float a;

- float b;

- Scanner myScanner = new Scanner(System.in);

- a = myScanner.nextFloat();

- b = myScanner.nextFloat();

- float a2 = a * a;

- float b2 = b * b;

- double c2 = a2 + b2;

- double c = Math.sqrt(c2);

- System.out.println("The square of a is: " + a2 + "
  The square of b is: " + b2 + " The square of c is: " +
  c2 + " C is: " + c);

- }

- }

Now, you are probably staring a bit wide-eyed at that one, wondering what it's all about so let's break it down.

The first line is different to what the original code read – what we are doing here is telling your program that you want it to import SCANNER, which is a Java utility. As you know, a scanner scans things and what it is going to do here is scan what you have input at the command line. With me so far?

float a; and float b; are both declaring variables and these require a floating point number – in simple terms, a number that has a decimal place in it, like 4.58. Remember this – int does not have any decimal places while float does.

Now things get a little but trickier.

Scanner myScanner = new Scanner(System.in) means that you have created a scanner that you imported and named it MYSCANNER. After that, you are using = to give it a value. (System.In) indicates that this is a new object and its input comes from System.In (the command line).

The line **a = myScanner.nextFloat();** is saying that variable a should be assigned to the first floating point number that the scanner reads. At that point, you input the number and press ENTER

The line **b = myScanner.nextFloat();** dos the same thing but with the next floating point number – again,input the number and press ETER

Now, there is quite a lot of mathematics in that piece of code:

- Float a2 = a * a; is declaring a variable with the name a2 and giving it a value that is the sum of variable a multiplied by the value of variable a

- Float b2 = b * b; is the same but with float b

- Double c2 = a2 + b2 declared a double accuracy number which is simply a long decimal number, and gives it a value of a2 plus b2

- Double c = Math.sqrt(c2); takes the root of c2 and then puts it in variable c

The final line of the code simply prints it all out. Anything inside the quote marks will be printed as text and the + gets used to combine the output. Anything that is not in the quotes will print the variable value

I am going to leave it there because, from here on it starts to get a lot more complicated and first you need to learn some of the functions of Java.

Chapter 13:
Java Functions

To understand what you are doing when you start to write your Java code, you must first understand the functions of Java. I already talked about some of the more basic ones earlier in this book so now it's time to look at some of the more advanced ones.

Loop Control

On occasion, you will need to execute one block of code multiple times. As a rule, all statements are executed in sequence, with the first in the function executed first, the second being executed second and so on to the end. Most programming languages have a number of control structures that allow you to have more complicated execution commands and Java is no exception.

Loop statements let you execute a single statement or a group of statements several times. The following is a list of the loops that Java provides to handle the looping requirements:

- **while loop** - will repeat a single or group of statements provided a given condition is true. The condition is tested before the loop body is executed

- **for loop** - will execute a statement sequence a number of times and will abbreviate the loop variable management code

- **do...while loop** – similar to the **while** statement, but with this one the condition is tested at the end of the loop body

Loop Control Statements

A loop control statement changes the execution sequence from its normal one As soon as the execution leaves a scope, all the automatic objects, created in the scope, will be destroyed. The following loop control statements are supported in Java:

- **break statement** – will terminate the switch or loop statement and execution will move to the statement that immediately follows it

- **continue statement** - makes the loop skip over the rest of the body and retest the condition before it starts again

Enhanced for loop

The enhanced for loop came in with Java 5 and is normally used to travel through a group of elements that may include arrays. The syntax used for the enhanced for loop is:

- for(declaration : expression)

- {

- //Statements

- }

Declaration is a block variable that is newly declared and is of a type that is fully compatible with all of the elements of the array that you are accessing. The variable is in the for block and it will have a value that is identical to current element in the array.

Expression is to evaluate to the array that you are looking to loop thorough and it can be either a method call that will return an array or it can be an array variable

For Example

- public class Test {
-
-    public static void main(String args[]){
-      int [] numbers = {10, 20, 30, 40, 50};
-
-      for(int x : numbers){
-       System.out.print(x);
-       System.out.print(",");
-      }
-      System.out.print("\n");
-      String [] names ={"James", "Larry", "Tom", "Lacy"};
-      for(String name : names) {
-       System.out.print(name);
-       System.out.print(",");
-      }
-    }
- }

Executing this code would give you this result:

- 10,20,30,40,50,

- James,Larry,Tom,Lacy

Numbers Class

In Java when we work with numbers, we normally use primitive data types, like double, int, byte, long, etc., for example:

- int i = 5000;

- float gpa = 13.65;

- byte mask = 0xaf;

However, occasionally in the development side of things, you may come across a situation where you would need to make use of an object instead, to do this, Java has something called **wrapper classes**. The wrapper classes are:

- Integer

- Long

- Byte

- Double

- Float

- Short

And they are subclasses of the main abstract number class.

The wrapper class contains primitive data types that, respective of its name, i.e. the Long wrapper class would contain long data types. Converting these primitive types into objects is known as boxing and the compiler does this for you. So, if you are using a wrapper class, all you need to do is pass the value of the data type inside it to the wrapper class constructer. The wrapper object is converted back into a primitive data type, in a process known as unboxing.

An example of boxing and unboxing would be:

- public class Test{
-
- public static void main(String args[]){
- Integer x = 5; // boxes int to an Integer object
- x = x + 10; // unboxes the Integer to a int
- System.out.println(x);
- }
- }

Executing this would give this result:

- 15

In a case where x is assigned an integer value, the compiler will box the integer because it is an object. A bit later on, x will be unboxed so it can be added in as an integer.

Number Methods

The following is a list of the instance methods that are implemented by all of the Number class subclasses:

- **xxxValue()** – converts the value of the number objet into data type xxx and returns i

- **compareTo()** – Compares the number object with the argument

- **equals()** - Will determine if the number object is, in fact, equal to the argument

- **valueOf()** - Will return an integer object that holds the value of the primitive that is specified

- **toString()** - Will return a String object that represents the value of the int or integer that is specified

- **parseInt()** - Is used to get the primitive data type of a specified String

- **abs()** - Will return the absolute value of the specified argument

- **ceil()** - Will return the smallest int that is equal to or larger than the argument and it will be returned as a double

- **floor()** - Will return the biggest int that is equal to or less than the argument and it will be retuned as a double

- **rint()** - Will return the int that has the closest value to the argument, also returned as a double

- **round()** - Will return the closest int or long, indicated by the type of the method return, to the argument

- **min()** - Will return the smallest of a pair of arguments

- **max()** - Will return the biggest of a pair of arguments

- **exp()** - Will return the natural logarithm base, for example, to the power of the argument

- **log()** - Will return the natural logarithm of the specified argument

- **pow()** - Will return the value of the leading argument, raised to the power of the next one

- **sqrt()** - Will return the square root of the specified argument

- **sin()** - will return the sine of the double value specified

- **cos()** - Will return the cosine of the double value specified

- **tan()** - Will return the tangent of the double value specified

- **asin()** - Will return the arcsine of the double value specified

- **acos()** - Will return the arccosine of the double value specified

- **atan()** - Will return the arctangent of the double value specified

- **atan2()** - Will convert rectangular co-ordinates to polar co-ordinates and will return theta (polar)

- **toDegrees()** - Will convert the argument into degrees

- **toRadians()** - Will convert the argument into radians

- **random()** - Will return a random number

Character Class

When we work with characters in Java, we tend to use the primitive data type called **char**, for example,

- char ch = 'a';
-
- // Unicode for uppercase Greek omega character
- char uniChar = '\u039A';
-
- // an array of chars
- char[] charArray ={ 'a', 'b', 'c', 'd', 'e' };

In the same way as we talked about with numbers, there is also a wrapper class called Character that allows you to use objects instead of the primitive data type char. There are a few very useful methods in the Character class that can be used for manipulation of characters and you can use the Character constructor to create a Character object, like this:

- Character ch = new Character('a');

There are some circumstances under which the compiler will create the Character object for you, for example, if you were to pass a primitive char to a method that is expecting an object, the compiler would convert the char to a

Character. This is known as auto boxing or, if the Character is converted to a char, it is known as unboxing.

For example:

- // Here following primitive char 'a'
- // is boxed into the Character object ch
- Character ch = 'a';
-
- // Here primitive 'x' is boxed for method test,
- // return is unboxed to char 'c'
- char c = test('x');

Escape Sequences

If a character is preceded by a (\) backslash, it is known as an escape sequence and has a special meaning to the compiler. You will probably have seen this (\n) in some programs as well. This is the newline character and is used mostly in System.out.printIn() statements to move on to the next line after printing the string. The following are the escape sequences in java:

- **\t** - Puts a tab into the text at the point marked

- **\b** - Puts a backspace into the text at the point marked

- **\n** - Puts a newline in the text at the point marked

- **\r** - Puts a carriage return in the text at the point marked

- **\f** - Puts a form feed in the text at the point marked

- \' - Puts a single quote character in the text at the point marked

- \" - Puts a double quote character in the text at the point marked

- \\ - Puts a backslash character in the text at the point marked

When the compiler comes across an escape sequence in a rint statement, it will interpret it as it is written.

For example, if you were to put quotes inside quotes, you would need to use the \" escape sequence on the inside quotes:

- public class Test {
-
- 　　public static void main(String args[]) {
- 　　　　System.out.println("She said \"Hello!\" to me.");
- 　　}
- }

Execution of this would produce this result:

- She said "Hello!" to me.

Character Methods

Below is a list of all the important instance methods that are implemented by the Character class subclasses:

- **isLetter()** – Will determine if the char value specified is a letter

- **isDigit()** – Will determine if the char value specified is a digit

- **isWhitespace()** – Will determine if the char value specified is white space

- **isUpperCase()** – Will determine if the char value specified is uppercase

- **isLowerCase()** - Will determine if the char value specified is lowercase

- **toUpperCase()** - Will return the specified char value in uppercase form

- **toLowerCase()** - Will return the specified char value in lowercase form

- **toString()** – Will return a String object that is a one-character String that represents the character value that is specified

Strings Class

Strings are used a lot in Java and they are simply a sequence of characters. Strings are known as objects in Java programming and the platform has the Strings class to allow you to create strings and manipulate them.

The easiest way to create a string is like this:

- String greeting = "Hello world!";

Whenever the compiler comes across a string literal written in your code, it will create a String object. In the case above, the value is "Hello, World!". Like any other object, String objects can be created with a constructor and the **new** keyword. There are 11 constructors in the String class and they all let you provide the starting value of the string through different course, like a character array. For example:

- public class StringDemo{
-
- public static void main(String args[]){
- char[] helloArray = { 'h', 'e', 'l', 'l', 'o', '.'};
- String helloString = new String(helloArray);
- System.out.println(helloString);
- }
- }

Executing this code would give this result:

- hello.

Be aware that the String class is immutable. This means that, once you have created it, you cannot change a String object. If you find that you need to modify character strings, you would need to use the classes, **String Buffer** and **string Builder.**

String Length

When you use a method to get information about an object, that method is called an accessor method. One that you can use is the **length()** method, which will return the number of characters that are inside the string object. For example:

- public class StringDemo {
-

```
public static void main(String args[]) {
    String palindrome = "Dot saw I was Tod";
    int len = palindrome.length();
    System.out.println( "String Length is : " + len );
}
}
```

Executing this code would produce this result:

- String Length is : 17

Concatenating Strings

There is a method in the String class for concatenating two strings:

- string1.concat(string2);

This will return a string that is string1 with the addition of string2 on the end of it. The concat() method can also be used with string literals, as such:

- "My name is ".concat("Zara");

Normally, we use the + operator to concatenate two strings:

- "Hello," + " world" + "!"

And the result of this would be:

- "Hello, world!"

For example:

- public class StringDemo {

- public static void main(String args[]) {
- String string1 = "saw I was ";
- System.out.println("Dot " + string1 + "Tod");
- }
- }

Execution of this code will give this result:

- Dot saw I was Tod

Creating Format Strings

To print the output with formatted numbers, you can use the printf() and the format() method. The equivalent in the string class is format() and his will return a String object instead of a PrintStream object. With the format() method, you can create a formatted string that is reusable, instead of a one-off.

For example, you could write this:

- System.out.printf("The value of the float variable is " +

  o "%f, while the value of the integer " +

  o "variable is %d, and the string " +

  o "is %s", floatVar, intVar, stringVar);

But, instead of that, you could write:

- String fs;

- fs = String.format("The value of the float variable is " +

- "%f, while the value of the integer " +

- "variable is %d, and the string " +

- "is %s", floatVar, intVar, stringVar);

- System.out.println(fs);

String Methods

Below is a list of all the methods that the String class supports:

- **char charAt(int index)** – returns the character at the index specified

- **int compareTo(Object o)** – Will compare the string to an object

- **int compareTo(String anotherString)** – will compare to strings lexicographically

- **int compareToIgnoreCase(String str)** – Will do the same as the above but will ignore any differences in the case

- **String concat(String str)** – Will concatenate the string that is specified to the end of this particular string

- **boolean contentEquals(StringBuffer sb)** – Will return true if, and only if, the string has the same sequence of characters as the StringBuffer that is specified

- **static String copyValueOf(char[] data)** – Will return a string that is representative of the sequence of characters in the specified array

- **static String copyValueOf(char[] data, int offset, int count)** – Does the same as the above method

- **boolean endsWith(String suffix)** – Will test if the string has the specified suffix on the end

- **boolean equals(Object anObject)** – Will compare this string to an object that is specified

- **boolean equalsIgnoreCase(String anotherString)** - Will compare one string to another but will ignore case considerations

- **byte getBytes()** – Will encode the string into a byte sequence, making use of the default charset and will store the result in a new array

- **byte[] getBytes(String charsetName** – Does the same as the above method

- **void getChars(int srcBegin, int srcEnd, char[] dst, int dstBegin)** – Will copy the characters from the string to the specified destination array

- **int hashCode()** – Will return a hash code

- **int indexOf(int ch)** – Will return the index in the string, of the first instance of the character specified

- **int indexOf(int ch, int fromIndex)** - As above but will start the search at the index specified

- **int indexOf(String str)** – Will return the index in the string of the first instance of the substring specified

- **int indexOf(String str, int fromIndex)** – As above but beginning the search at the index specified

- **String intern()** – Will return a canonical representation

- **int lastIndexOf(int ch)** – Will return the index in the string with the last instance of the character specified

- **int lastIndexOf(int ch, int fromIndex)** – As above but beginning the search at the specified index and searching backwards

- **int lastIndexOf(String str)** – Will return the index in the string of the rightmost instance of the substring specified

- **int lastIndexOf(String str, int fromIndex)** – Will return the index in the string of the last instance of the substring specified but will search backwards from the index specified

- **int length()** – Wil return the length of the string

- **boolean matches(String regex)** – will tell you whether the string matches a specified regular expression

- **boolean regionMatches(boolean ignoreCase, int toffset, String other, int ooffset, int len)** – Will test to see if two string regions are equal to one another

- **boolean regionMatches(int toffset, String other, int ooffset, int len)** – Does the same as the above method

- **String replace(char oldChar, char newChar)** – Will return a new string that is the result of replacing all instances of oldChar with newChar

- **String replaceAll(String regex, String replacement** – Will replace each substring of the string that matches a specified regular expression with a specified replacement

- **String replaceFirst(String regex, String replacement)** – Will replace the first substring of the index that matches with a specified regular expression with the specified replacement

- **String[] split(String regex)** – Will split the string around any matches of a specified regular expression

- **String[] split(String regex, int limit)** – Does the same as the above method

- **boolean startsWith(String prefix)** – Will test to see if the string begins with the prefix specified

- **boolean startsWith(String prefix, int toffset)** – As above but tests to see if the prefix begins a specified index

- **CharSequence subSequence(int beginIndex, int endIndex)** – Will return a character sequence that is a subsequence of the sequence

- **String substring(int beginIndex)** – Will return a new string that is a substring of the string

- **String substring(int beginIndex, int endIndex)** – Does the same as the above method

- **char[] toCharArray()** – Will convert the string into a character array

- **String toLowerCase()** – Will convert the characters in the string into lowercase, making use of the default locale rules

- **String toLowerCase(Locale locale)** – As above, using the specified locale rules

- **String toString()** – The string returns itself

- **String toUpperCase()** – This will convert the characters that are in this string to upper case, making use of the default locale rules

- **String toUpperCase(Locale locale)** – As above but using the specified locale rules

- **String trim()** – Will return a copy of the string, omitting the leading and the trailing whitespace

- **static String valueOf(primitive data type x)** – Will return the representation of the argument that is passed data type

Arrays

Arrays are also used a lot in Java and these store a sequence of fixed-size elements that are all the same type. Arrays store data collections but it is more often that an array if thought of as a collection of variables that are the same type.

Instead of individual variables, you would declare one array variable with individual variables represented inside.

Declaring Array Variables

If you want to use an array, you first have to declare a variable. This is to reference the array and you must specify which type of array the variable is able to reference. To declare an array variable, you would use this syntax:

- dataType[] arrayRefVar; // preferred way.

- or

- dataType arrayRefVar[];   //   works but not preferred way.

For example:

- double[] myList;   // preferred way.

- or

- double myList[];   // works but not preferred
  way.

Creating Arrays

To create an array with the new operator, use this syntax:

- arrayRefVar = new dataType[arraySize];

This statement is doing two things:

- It uses the dataType[arraySize] to create an array

- The reference of the array is assigned to the variable arrayRefVar

You can declare an array variable, create a new array and assign the reference to the variable using just one statement, like this:

- dataType[] arrayRefVar = new dataType[arraySize];

Or you can do this:

- dataType[] arrayRefVar = {value0, value1, ..., valuek};

The index is used to access the array elements and the indices are 0-based, which means that they begin from 0 to **arrayRefVar.length-1**.

For example:

This statement shows an array variable being declared, called myList, an array consisting of 10 elements created, all of double type and the reference assigned to myList:

- double[] myList = new double[10];

Processing Arrays

When we process array elements, we tend to use the for loop or the foreach loop simply because all of the elements are the same type and we know what the array size is. The following example shows you how to create an array, initialize it and then process it:

```java
public class TestArray {
public static void main(String[] args) {
double[] myList = {1.9, 2.9, 3.4, 3.5};
// Print all the array elements
for (int i = 0; i < myList.length; i++) {
System.out.println(myList[i] + " ");
}
// Summing all elements
double total = 0;
for (int i = 0; i < myList.length; i++) {
total += myList[i];
}
System.out.println("Total is " + total);
// Finding the largest element
double max = myList[0];
for (int i = 1; i < myList.length; i++) {
if (myList[i] > max) max = myList[i];
}
System.out.println("Max is " + max);
}
}
```

Executing this code would give this result:

- 1.9

- 2.9

- 3.4

- 3.5

- Total is 11.7

- ax is 3.5

The foreach Loops

The foreach loop came in with JDK 1.5. This allows you to travel through the entire array in sequence without needing to resort to the use of an index variable

For example:

This code shows all of the elements that are in the myList array:

- public class TestArray {
- public static void main(String[] args) {
- double[] myList = {1.9, 2.9, 3.4, 3.5};
- // Print all the array elements
- for (double element: myList) {
- System.out.println(element);
- }
- }
- }

Executing the code would give this result:

- 1.9

- 2.9

- 3.4

- 3.5

Passing Arrays to Methods

In the same way that we pass primitive data type values to methods, we can pass an array to a method. The following example is a method showing the elements that are in an int array:

- public static void printArray(int[] array) {
- for (int i = 0; i < array.length; i++) {
- System.out.print(array[i] + " ");
- }
- }

To invoke it we would pass an array, for example, the statement in the example below would invoke the printArray method:

- printArray(new int[]{3, 1, 2, 6, 4, 2});

The result of this would be:

- 3, 1, 2, 6, 4, 2;

Returning an Array from a Method

Methods are also able to return arrays and, in the example shown below, the method returns an array that is simply the reversal of another one:

- public static int[] reverse(int[] list) {
- int[] result = new int[list.length];
- for (int i = 0, j = result.length - 1; i < list.length; i++, j--) {
- result[j] = list[i];
- }
- return result;
- }

The Arrays Class

In the jave.util.Arays class, there are several static methods that allow you to search and sort arrays, compare them and fill the elements. The following is a list of the methods:

- **public static int binarySearch(Object[] a, Object key)** – Will search for a specified value, in a specified object array, using the binary search algorithm. Before this call is made, the array must be sorted. The search key index will be returned, provided it is in the list, otherwise the return will be (-(insertion point +1)

- **, public static boolean equals(long[] a, long[] a2),** - Will return true if both of the specified arrays are equal to each other. Two arrays are equal if both have the same number of elements and the corresponding element pairs in the arrays are equal. This will return true if both arrays are equal. The same method can be used by all data types.

- **public static void fill(int[] a, int val)** – Will assign the int value that is specified to an array of ints that is also specified.

- **public static void sort(Object[] a)** – Will sort the specified array into ascending order, going by the ordering of the elements

Date and Time

The java.util package contains the Date class, which encloses the date and time. There are two constructors that are supported by the class:

- **Date** – initializes the object with the date and time

- **Date (long millisec)** – Accepts an argument that is equal to the number of milliseconds that have passed since midnight on January 1 1970.

The list below details the methods supported by the Date class:

- **boolean after(Date date)** – Will return true if the Date object that is invoking has a later date than the specified one. If not, it will return False

- **boolean before(Date date)** – Same as the above method

- **Object clone( )** – Will duplicate the invoking Date object

- **int compareTo(Date date)** – Will compare the value of the invoking object with the value of Date. If the values are equal, it will return 0. If the invoking object is before the Date object, False is returned, while True will be returned if it is later.

- **int compareTo(Object obj)** – Exactly the same as the above method, provide the obj is of the Date class. If not, a ClassCastException will be thrown up

- **boolean equals(Object date)** – Will return true if the invoking Date object has the same date and time as the specified one, otherwise false will be returned

- **long getTime( )** – Will return the number of milliseconds that have passed by since January 1, 1970

- **int hashCode( )** – Will return a hash code for the invoking object

- **void setTime(long time)** – Will set the date and time as specified by time, representing the time elapsed in milliseconds since midnight, January 1, 1970

- **String toString( )** – Will convert the invoking object to a string and the return the result

Getting the Current Date & Time

This is very easy to do; all you need is a simple date object, together with the *toString()* method, as the example shows:

- import java.util.Date;
- public class DateDemo {
- public static void main(String args[]) {
- // Instantiate a Date object
- Date date = new Date();
- // display time and date using toString()
- System.out.println(date.toString());
- }
- }

This would give this result:

- on May 04 09:51:52 CDT 2009

Date Comparison

There are three ways in Java to compare dates:

- Use **getTime()** to find out the number of milliseconds that have passed since midnight on January 1, 1970. E this for both objects and then compare the values

- Use the **before()**, **after()** and **equals()** methods. For example, because the 12th day of the month is before the 18th day, **newDate(99, 2, 12).before(newDate (99, 2, 18)** would return true

- Use the **compareTo()** method

Date Formatting using SimpleDateFormat

SimpleDateFormat is known as a concrete class for both formatting and parsing dates. It allows you to choose any

118

pattern that is user-defined for date and time formatting, as such:

- import java.util.*;
- import java.text.*;
- public class DateDemo {
- public static void main(String args[]) {
- Date dNow = new Date( );
- SimpleDateFormat ft =
- new SimpleDateFormat ("E yyyy.MM.dd 'at' hh:mm:ss a zzz");
- System.out.println("Current Date: " + ft.format(dNow));
- }
- }

Executing this would give this result:

- Current Date: Sun 2004.07.18 at 04:14:09 PM PDT

Simple DateFormat format codes

In order to specify a time format, you would use a time pattern string. All ASCII letters are reserved int his string as pattern letters and these are defined as such:

Character	Description	Example
G	Era Designator	AD
Y	Year in 4 digits	2000
M	Month in the Year	May or 05

d	Day in the month	11
h	Hour in the AM or PM (1-12)	12
H	Hour in the day (0-23)	21
m	Minute in the hour	30
s	Second in the minute	53
S	Millisecond	258
E	Day in the week	Wednesday
D	Day in the year	342
F	Day of the week in the month	2 (second Thursday in May)
w	Week in the year	25
W	Week in the month	2
a	AM or PM marker	AM
k	Hour in the day (1-24)	22
K	Hour in the AM or PM (0-11)	9
z	Time zone	GMT
'	Escape for text	Delimiter

"	Single quote	'

Date Formatting using printf

It is very easy to format the date and time with the printf method. All you do is use a wo-leer format that starts with **t** and ends in one of the letters above. For example:

- import java.util.Date;
- public class DateDemo {
- public static void main(String args[]) {
- // Instantiate a Date object
- Date date = new Date();
- // display time and date using toString()
- String str = String.format("Current Date/Time : %tc", date);
- System.out.printf(str);
- }
- }

Executing this code would give this result:

- Current Date/Time : Sat Dec 15 16:37:57 MST 2012

To avoid having to give the date several times over to format each part, you can use a format string to indicate which index is to be formatted:

The index has to follow the % and it has to be terminated by a $. For example:

- import java.util.Date;
- public class DateDemo {

- public static void main(String args[]) {
- // Instantiate a Date object
- Date date = new Date();

- // display time and date using toString()
- System.out.printf("%1$s %2$tB %2$td, %2$tY",
- "Due date:", date);
- }
- }

This would give this result

- Due date: February 09, 2004

You could, if you wanted to, use the < flag, which indicates that the argument that was in the preceding format specification should be used again, for example:

- import java.util.Date;
- public class DateDemo {
- public static void main(String args[]) {
- // Instantiate a Date object
- Date date = new Date();
- // display formatted date
- System.out.printf("%s %tB %<te, %<tY",
- "Due date:", date);
- }
- }

And this would give this result:

- Due date: February 09, 2004

Parsing Strings into Dates

There are some other methods in the SimpleDateFormat class, most importantly parse(), which will parse a string going on the format that is stored in the object. For example:

- import java.util.*;
- import java.text.*;
- public class DateDemo {
- public static void main(String args[]) {
- SimpleDateFormat ft = new SimpleDateFormat ("yyyy-MM-dd");
- String input = args.length == 0 ? "1818-11-11" : args[0];
- System.out.print(input + " Parses as ");
- Date t;
- try {
- t = ft.parse(input);
- System.out.println(t);
- } catch (ParseException e) {
- System.out.println("Unparseable using " + ft);
- }
- }
- }

If you ran the above code, you would get this result:

- $ java DateDemo

- 1818-11-11 Parses as Wed Nov 11 00:00:00 GMT 1818

- $ java DateDemo 2007-12-01

- 2007-12-01 Parses as Sat Dec 01 00:00:00 GMT 2007

Sleeping for a Time

You can set your program to sleep from one millisecond right up to the lifespan of the computer. The following example shows a program that would sleep for a period of 10 seconds

- import java.util.*;
- public class SleepDemo {
- public static void main(String args[]) {
- try {
- System.out.println(new Date( ) + "\n");
- Thread.sleep(5*60*10);
- System.out.println(new Date( ) + "\n");
- } catch (Exception e) {
- System.out.println("Got an exception!");
- }
- }
- }

Running this program would produce this result:

- Sun May 03 18:04:41 GMT 2009

- Sun May 03 18:04:51 GMT 2009

Measuring Elapsed Time

On occasion, you might need to measure time in milliseconds, particularly point in time. The above example can be rewritten as:

- import java.util.*;
- public class DiffDemo {
- public static void main(String args[]) {
- try {
- long start = System.currentTimeMillis( );
- System.out.println(new Date( ) + "\n");
- Thread.sleep(5*60*10);
- System.out.println(new Date( ) + "\n");
- long end = System.currentTimeMillis( );
- long diff = end - start;
- System.out.println("Difference is : " + diff);
- } catch (Exception e) {
- System.out.println("Got an exception!");
- }
- }
- }

And executing this would give this result:

- Sun May 03 18:16:51 GMT 2009

- Sun May 03 18:16:57 GMT 2009

- Difference is : 5993

GregorianCalendar Class

The GregorianCalendar is known as a concrete implementation of a class that implements the familiar Gregorian calendar. Using the **getInstance**() method in the Calendar class would return the GregorianCalendar, initialized with the date and time in the time zone and default locale. There are two fields defined in GregorianCalendar – AD and BC. These are representative of the eras that are defined by the GregorianCalendar. There are a number of constructs that are supported by GregorianCalendar objects:

- **GregorianCalendar()** – Constructs a Gregoriancalendar that uses the current time and the default locale in the default time zone

- **GregorianCalendar(int year, int month, int date)** – Uses a specified date with the default locales and time zone

- **GregorianCalendar(int year, int month, int date, int hour, int minute)** – Does the same as above

- **GregorianCalendar(int year, int month, int date, int hour, int minute, int second)** – Does the same as above

- **GregorianCalendar(Locale aLocale)** – Uses the current time with a specified locale in the default time zone

- **GregorianCalendar(TimeZone zone)** – Uses the current time in a specified time zone and the default locale

- **GregorianCalendar(TimeZone zone, Locale aLocale)** – Uses the current time in a specified time zone and the specified locale

Below is a list of some of the more useful support methods that the GregorianCalendar class provides:

- **void add(int field, int amount)** – Will add the specified time to the specified field, using the rules of the calendar

- **protected void computeFields()** – Will convert UTC from milliseconds to time field values

- **protected void computeTime()** – Will override the Calendar and convert UTC from time field values to milliseconds

- **boolean equals(Object obj)** – Will make comparisons between the GregorianCalendar and a specified object reference

- **int get(int field)** – Will obtain the value for a specified time field

- **int getActualMaximum(int field)** – Will return the maximum value possible for this field, going on the specified date

- **int getActualMinimum(int field)** – Will return the minimum value possible for the filed using the current date

- **int getGreatestMinimum(int field)** – Will return the highest minimum value for the specified field if varies

- **Date getGregorianChange()** – Will get the GregorianCalendar to change date

- **int getLeastMaximum(int field)** – Will return the lowest of the maxmum values for the specified field if varies

- **int getMaximum(int field)** – Will return the maximum possible value for the specified field

- **Date getTime()** – Will get the current time for the calendar

- **long getTimeInMillis()** – Will return the current time on the calendar as a long

- **TimeZone getTimeZone()** – Will return the time zone

- **int getMinimum(int field)** – Will return the minimum value for a specified field

- **int hashCode()** – Will override the hash code

- **boolean isLeapYear(int year)** – Will determine if the specified year is a leap year

- **void roll(int field, boolean up)** – Will add or subtract a single time unit on the specified field without making changes to larger fields

- **void set(int field, int value)** – Wil set the time field with the specified value

- **void set(int year, int month, int date)** – Will set the values for the year, month and date fields

- **void set(int year, int month, int date, int hour, int minute)** – Will set the value for the year, month, date, hours and minutes fields

- **void set(int year, int month, int date, int hour, int minute, int second)** – Will set the values for the year, month, date, hours, minutes and seconds fields

- **void setGregorianChange(Date date)** – Will set the GregorianCalendar to change date

- **void setTime(Date date)** – Will set the current time on the Calendar with the specified date

- **void setTimeInMillis(long millis)** – Will set the current time on the Calendar from the specified long value

- **void setTimeZone(TimeZone value)** – Will set the time zone with the specified time zone value

- **String toString()** – Will return a string representation of the Calendar

Here is the list of few useful support methods provided by GregorianCalendar class:

For Example:

- import java.util.*;
- public class GregorianCalendarDemo {
- public static void main(String args[]) {
- String months[] = {
- "Jan", "Feb", "Mar", "Apr",
- "May", "Jun", "Jul", "Aug",
- "Sep", "Oct", "Nov", "Dec"};

- int year;
- // Create a Gregorian calendar initialized
- // with the current date and time in the

- // default locale and timezone.
- GregorianCalendar gcalendar = new GregorianCalendar();
- // Display current time and date information.
- System.out.print("Date: ");
- System.out.print(months[gcalendar.get(Calendar.MONTH)]);
- System.out.print(" " + gcalendar.get(Calendar.DATE) + " ");
- System.out.println(year = gcalendar.get(Calendar.YEAR));
- System.out.print("Time: ");
- System.out.print(gcalendar.get(Calendar.HOUR) + ":");
- System.out.print(gcalendar.get(Calendar.MINUTE) + ":");
- System.out.println(gcalendar.get(Calendar.SECOND));
- // Test if the current year is a leap year
- if(gcalendar.isLeapYear(year)) {
- System.out.println("The current year is a leap year");
- }
- else {
- System.out.println("The current year is not a leap year");
- }
- }
- }

If you ran this program, it would produce this result:

- Date: Apr 22 2009

- Time: 11:25:27

- The current year is not a leap year

Conclusion

With this, we have come to the end of this handbook on learning Java. I sincerely hope you enjoyed this session and were able to learn and understand the programming. As you can see, it looks complicated to the untrained eye and the unpracticed mind. However, once you start and once you understand the basics, you will find yourself programming the days away!

I thank you for choosing this book. Happy learning!

www.ingramcontent.com/pod-product-compliance
Lightning Source LLC
Chambersburg PA
CBHW071252050326
40690CB00011B/2371